My Mind's Eye

A Collection of Poems

by

Ra'Shell S. Maldon

Published by:

B.O.S.S. Publishing, LLC

General Information

My Mind's Eye
Ra'Shell S. Maldon

All Rights Reserved. No part of this publication may be reproduced, stored in a retrieval system, or transmitted, in any form or in any means – by electronic, mechanical, photocopying, recording or otherwise – without prior written permission of the "Material Owner" or its Representative **B.O.S.S. Publishing, LLC**. Any such violation infringes upon the Creative and Intellectual Property of the Owner pursuant to International and Federal Copyright Law. Any queries pertaining to this "Collection" should be addressed to Publisher of Record.

Copyright © 2017: Ra'Shell S. Maldon

Cover Design: Greg Tellis

Publisher: B.O.S.S. Publishing, LLC

Editor: Terry L. Ware Sr.

ISBN: 978-0-9988341-1-5

1. Poetry

First Edition

Credits

Author
Ra'Shell S. Maldon

Book Cover Design by:
Greg Tellis

gregtellisdesign.com

Dedication

For the weary souls wandering in the dark.

Allow my light to illuminate your path.

Preface

My Mind's Eye is an extension of who I am and what I stand for. It is the product of not only my efforts, but also my growth as a poet and a woman. Comprised of thirty poems, this book provides insight into my thought process and my experiences concerning the emotional, mental, physical, and spiritual aspects of life. Amidst the process of completing this book, I have found and embraced my voice as well as my light. And I am thankful for the opportunity to share both with you.

While reading each poem, I encourage you to receive the energy behind my words and perceive their significance. After reading each poem, my hope is for you to obtain a better understanding not merely of me, but also of yourself.

Peace and Positivity

Ra'Shell Maldon

Foreword

It takes talent to be able to express yourself about what life has brought you & taught you. It takes courage to allow yourself to be vulnerable to the possible criticism that may come from your interpretation. It takes will to be able to say this is what I will do and say to get my point, my experiences, and my vision across to the world.

When an individual is able to compose words that we utilize in our daily lives and expresses them in a way that pulls us into that very moment, we can say without speaking, how immediately connected we are. The words that are expressed by Ra'Shell are truly just that, a connection.

Explore her thoughts, feel her emotions, but most of all enjoy the connection.)

Isaac "IkeGreenTea" Crawford

Table of Contents

Dedication |pg. iv

Preface |pg. v

Foreword |pg. vi

Part One:
Consciously Speaking to My People |pg. 1

Chapter One:
Public Service Announcement |pg. **2**

Chapter Two:
No Disrespect |pg. **5**

Table of Contents.... continued

Chapter Three:

Ill-Informed King | pg. **9**

Chapter Four:

Queen Recognize Queen | pg. **11**

Chapter Five:

Interceder | pg. **14**

Chapter Six:

Public Service Announcement II | pg. **17**

Chapter Seven:

R is for Revolutionary | pg. **20**

Chapter Eight:

ill b.k.a. Innocence Long Lost | pg. **25**

Chapter Nine:

Addict to Addict | pg. **30**

Table of Contents.... continued

Chapter Ten:

Solicited Reprobation | pg. **33**

Chapter Eleven:

Public Service Announcement III | pg. **35**

Chapter Twelve:

Zion Train | pg. **37**

Chapter Thirteen:

Chin Up | pg. **40**

Chapter Fourteen:

Pushing Consistency | pg. **43**

Chapter Fifteen:

S is for Survivor | pg. **47**

Table of Contents.... continued

Part Two:
Consciously Seeking for Myself |pg. 49

Chapter Sixteen:

sis b.k.a. Still I Strive |pg. **51**

Chapter Seventeen:

My World Asunder |pg. **54**

Chapter Eighteen:

This Woman's Growth |pg. **56**

Chapter Nineteen:

No Cry |pg. **58**

Chapter Twenty:

Misconception of Words |pg. **61**

Table of Contents.... continued

Chapter Twenty-One:

Breezes | pg. **65**

Chapter Twenty-Two:

Sometimes | pg. **67**

Chapter Twenty-Three:

Expired Possibility | pg. **70**

Chapter Twenty-Four:

Self-Destruction | pg. **75**

Chapter Twenty-Five:

Sea of Insecurities | pg. **78**

Chapter Twenty-Six:

Destruction of a Broken-Hearted Soul | pg. **81**

Chapter Twenty-Seven:

Creation to Creator | pg. **84**

Table of Contents.... continued

Chapter Twenty-Eight:
Destination (Reconciliation or Separation) |pg. **88**

Chapter Twenty-Nine:
Free Fall (Free for All) |pg. **93**

Chapter Thirty:
lol b.k.a Longing Out Loud |pg. **95**

Author's Address |pg. 96
Connections to Ra'Shell |pg. 97
Author's Q&A |pg. 98

Ra'Shell S. Maldon

My Mind's Eye

A Collection of Poems

by

Ra'Shell S. Maldon

Published by:

B.O.S.S. Publishing, LLC

Ra'Shell S. Maldon

Part One:

Consciously Speaking to My People

Chapter One:

Public Service Announcement

Ra'Shell S. Maldon

We were created

In our Creator's image

Ordained to reign like kings and queens

Or gods and goddesses

Conditioned to believe that we are powerless

We remain unaware of the power

That was instilled within us from birth

So we underestimate our worth

And are encouraged to believe that we are inferior

Discriminated against because of the melanin that covers our exterior

We are discouraged from tapping into the spirit

Embedded within our interior

For we have exchanged our spirituality for their religion

And we have lost sight of our ancestors' vision

We are still sleeping I suppose

And no one knows

When we are going to awaken

And stop buying the dreams we were being sold

Start seeking knowledge for ourselves

My Mind's Eye

And stop accepting the lies we are being told.

Chapter Two:

No Disrespect

My Mind's Eye

Sistas no disrespect

But if we neglect

To respect ourselves

Then we can't expect a man to

I'm fully aware of how some of you do

On a night out with the crew

You dress as though you're seeking someone to screw

But sistas over-stand

You don't have to dress

For easy access

To attract the attention of a man

In retrospect

I can admit that I have been a guilty suspect

Of revealing a bit of skin

Every now and again

But out of respect for myself

I learned to leave something to the imagination

Realizing that if I respect myself first

Then a man will respect me second without hesitation

But apparently self-respect

Ra'Shell S. Maldon

Is a foreign concept

That you simple-minded sistas lack

Leaving many to assume

That you never learned how to be good at something other than lying on your back

So you continue to project the wrong impression

Falling victim to the misconception

That you're a whore

And a causal fuck is the only thing you're good for

You can't fault any man for assuming that

Especially when your outfit is so short it exposes your cat

Every time your song comes on

And you pussy pop

Sistas stop

Have some dignity have some class

A man would respect you

If you didn't expose your ass

He'll respect you every time

If you only stimulate his mind

By exposing your intellect

My Mind's Eye

But if you only stimulate his body

Here's a breakdown of exactly what you'll get:

Maybe his tongue

Definitely his prick

He'll bust a nut

And shortly after he'll split

With no intent to commit

Leaving you feeling disrespected

But the blame isn't on him

The blame is on you

Because since you neglected to respect yourself first

He didn't feel the need to.

Chapter Three:

Ill-Informed King

My Mind's Eye

Unaware of your history

Diminishing the mystery as to why you fall victim to the stereotype

You are the type

To praise peasants and temporal things

But shun eternal things

And disrespect queens while neglecting to father your offspring

You remain stuck on tradition

And you stay on a money-making mission to replicate what you see on TV

Blind to the reality that you were born king

So unknowingly you hide your crown under fitted hats

Nobody ever taught you to do better

Thus, as a result, you never thought to do better

And you never learned to be royalty so remain a servant

Rather a slave to the lies you are being sold.

Chapter Four:

Queen Recognize Queen

My Mind's Eye

She has the type of legs that open easily
And it displeases me
To know that she's unaware of her worth
She's been a queen since the day of her birth
Although she doesn't carry herself as such
For me it's a bit much
To think of the countless men
She's allowed to invade her temple
Oh how it hurts my mental
To see her disrespect
And neglect to love herself
She's playing Russian roulette with her health
And she doesn't even know it
She's just chasing a feeling
In dire need of spiritual healing
But she rejects anything spiritual
Still I preach to her
Hoping my lectures will reach to her
And teach her how to transition from irresponsible fiend

Ra'Shell S. Maldon

To responsible queen.

Chapter Five:

Interceder

Ra'Shell S. Maldon

I tell her

That I love her

As often as I feel she needs to hear it

In hopes that my sincerity

Is enough to guide her spirit

To the clarity

That she often seeks

But rarely does she find

At times, I tire myself mentally

Trying to decipher the chaos in her mind

Because it saddens me

To witness her embracing the company

Of misery

As though she doesn't have friends and family

To rely on

Still for her sake

I keep my shoulder on standby

For her to cry on

If ever she needs it

Telling her to bear in mind

My Mind's Eye

That no matter the time
Whenever she's ready to talk
I'm ready to listen
And hoping that our Maker
Will readily incline His ear to listen
To every petition
That my spirit intercedes
On her behalf.

Chapter Six:

Public Service Announcement II

My Mind's Eye

My people wake up

Because while you were sleeping

Our oppressor was creeping

Into you mind

Planting various seeds at a time

Instilling inferiority and jealousy with intent to keep that crab mentality intact

To keep us blind to the fact

That our prosperity has been hindered

Our identity has been surrendered

Leaving rendered defenseless against mental warfare

The system was designed to impair

Our judgements so that we remain unaware

Of the power in unity

As a result

We often lack a sense of community

So divided that we kill each other when we should be killing oppression

And applying aggression

To teaching and reaching our youth

Exposing them to the truth

Ra'Shell S. Maldon

So that they aren't susceptible to believe the lies we've been told

Nor buy the dreams we've been sold

My people wake up

Because you've been sleeping too long.

Chapter Seven:

R is for Revolutionary

Ra'Shell S. Maldon

He said that he's going to be a revolutionary

Racism still exists

He says

The system is corrupt

He says

It's designed for us to fail

We aren't the only ones oppressed

But we are the ones affected the worst

He says

As he speaks his truth

I'm inclined to listen

And I'm inclined to inquire

About the significance of his cause and why it inspires

Him to become a revolutionary

He longs to undo what has been done

He says

Civil rights activists may have settled for something

But their battle has yet to be won

He says

As he speaks his truth

My Mind's Eye

I'm inclined to believe

That together we can achieve

Something so profound

As reviving our dignity that lies between

Our oppressor's feet and the ground

The more he speaks

The more I'm inclined to be down for his revolution

And I'm inclined to play my role

In being a part of the solution

Rather the problem

Fully aware that his revolution isn't enough

To resolve every problem

But it is a start

To bring awareness and awaken our thought

He says

That he'd rather be assassinated than imprisoned

And I reply

That I've been a prisoner

In my mind

And I've been a prisoner

Ra'Shell S. Maldon

In this world
So I know firsthand that prison isn't fit
For kings and queens to sit
On this we both agree
So when the opposition comes
To bring the reign of his revolution to a close
We won't go quietly
But we will go fighting
Before reuniting
With the revolutionaries who fought before us
No, we won't go compliantly
But we will go defiantly
Standing firm on our beliefs
We will draw our weapons and shoot
At our oppressors
Knowing that they will shoot back
With intent to kill
Causing our courage to spill
Allowing us to feel
The sun

My Mind's Eye

With one last look into his third eye
I say that I
Vow to be by his side
When the bullets cease to fly
And when the smoke ceases to cloud the sky
I know that I
Will be honored to die
Next to this revolutionary.

Chapter Eight:

ill b.k.a. Innocence Long Lost

My Mind's Eye

An intervention is needed
But the hope that her family harbors within
Inevitably depletes
Until they find themselves undoubtedly accepting defeat
As the gravity
Of their harsh reality
Begins to hit
That they cannot help
Someone who refuses to commit
To being helped
Her darkest secrets she kept hidden from the view
Of the individuals who matter
Those who would rather
She be healthy
Instead of buried six feet underneath the dirt
Even from a distance
Her loved ones can sense her hurt
And it is from a distance
That they worry and wonder

Ra'Shell S. Maldon

About the occurrences that trigger her self-esteem to shatter
Then retreat into hiding
So that her logic is no longer siding
With rationality
But is consumed by the irrationality
That her existence
Should no longer exist
And that if she committed suicide her existence
Would no longer be missed
At least through the eyes
Of anyone on the outside looking in
That is precisely the way she has been behaving
Carrying on as though her existence
Is unworthy of saving
For she consistently ignores
Her liver's craving
For substance
More fulfilling than the substance
That has been filling

My Mind's Eye

And killing her throughout the years

Closed mindedness suggesting that she cower inside of her fears

She nearly drowns

While swimming inside a sea of her tears

Because she is preoccupied with the insatiable appetite

Of her flesh

Misleading her to assume

That the alcohol she frequently consumes

Is the best

Remedy to lay her burdens

Down to rest

So she pours her own poison daily

Red or white wine

She has no preference lately

Dark or light liquor

She drinks beyond her tolerance

To alleviate her pain quicker

While disregarding the reality

That each drink leaves her body sicker

Ra'Shell S. Maldon

Still she absorbs alcohol until her taste buds
Lose their sense of taste
Because she remains unwilling to face
The underlying issues that trace
The confines
Of her feeble spirit and her childlike mind.

Chapter Nine:

Addict to Addict

Ra'Shell S. Maldon

I tried not to preach

To her

But my speech

To her

Was always blunt

In hopes that my truth

Would penetrate deep into the gut

Of her soul

Like the edge of a sharpened shank

To her

I uttered the type

Of truth aimed to make

Her thank

Our Maker that He

Didn't see fit

For her to experience

The trials and tribulations

I endured then overcame with resilience

Uncertain as to whether or not

She was paying attention

My Mind's Eye

But to her

The last truth I decided to mention

Was that we're both addicts

In reality

The difference is my addiction

Heightens my clarity

While her addiction

Devours then diminishes her being

Until the meaning

Of her existence becomes irrelevant

In her mind.

Ra'Shell S. Maldon

Chapter Ten:

Solicited Reprobation

My Mind's Eye

The religion orchestrated

By our downpressors

Then force fed

To our ancestors

Is still being spoon fed

And spread

With intent to mislead

Miseducate

Then impede our spiritual growth

Blinding us

To the value of our spirituality's worth

As our downpressors perpetuate

The inevitable fate

That awaits

Misguided souls.

Chapter Eleven:

Public Service Announcement III

My Mind's Eye

Foolish pride
Will forever divide
The boastful from the meek
The strong from the weak
And the misguided from the wise
Open your eyes
You're still sleeping
While melanated mothers are still weeping
And still mourning the loss
Of their sons who were lost
In the system or lost in the streets
Why are still sleeping
When melanated mothers are still weeping
And still mourning the loss
Of their sons who lost
Their lives to senseless violence
Stop sleeping
And lift your eyelids.

Chapter Twelve:

Zion Train

My Mind's Eye

I see Zion train

Approaching in the distance

I see Zion train

Advocating soul salvation with persistence

The emancipation of our people

Is at hand

The evacuation of our people

Has been planned

I see Zion train

Approaching in the distance

Your ticket is your heart's intent

Your ticket is your willingness to repent

Too many of our years have been spent

Spellbound and down pressed

Too many tears of lament have been spilt

Over countless lives our down pressers have kilt

I see Zion train

Approaching in the distance

Relinquish your spiritual shackles

And reclaim your rightful place

Ra'Shell S. Maldon

I see Zion train
Approaching in the distance
Relinquish your mental shackles
And occupy a righteous space
Where we no longer have to
Be their chattel
We no longer have to
Endure their slaughter like cattle
And we no longer have to
Live in fear
For Zion train is drawing near.

Chapter Thirteen:

Chin Up

Ra'Shell S. Maldon

Sometimes what doesn't kill you
Makes me want to
Kill yourself
Until you rationalize
That the selfishness of this flesh
Isn't worth the compromise
Of morale
That opposes the notion
Of leaving loved ones behind
With sorrow filled eyes
And unspoken goodbyes
The weight
Of such consequence
Is far too great
Undetermined fate
Yet you're determined to wait
Without a specific date in mind
You anticipate the time
When your mind
Is unbiased to see clearly

My Mind's Eye

That better days
Aren't as distant as they appear
Because when you've been down for so long
There's nowhere
Left to go from there except up.

Ra'Shell S. Maldon

Chapter Fourteen:

Pushing Consistency

My Mind's Eye

Lately

I've been pushing consistency

And shedding the weight

Consistently

Like a neighborhood pusher

But I'm no pusher

Well

At least not really

I'm merely

Pushing myself

To do better

And be better

That is all

Still they call

Upon me

Whenever they see me

Like a fiend in search of a foreign fix

Approaching almost in secrecy

Seeking the secret

To shedding the weight

Ra'Shell S. Maldon

As though my answer will somehow reveal

Guidance on how

To achieve the favorable results

That they seek

So to them I speak

About the effects of allowing my mind's eye

To occupy

A space in an optimistic state

That ultimately

Grants me the clarity

To find

The endurance necessary

To carry

Myself through

Empowering me to continue

To strive

As these goals of mine

Realign into proper perspective

Motivating me

To push myself to be

My Mind's Eye

Physically and mentally active
Consistently.

Chapter Fifteen:

S is for Survivor

My Mind's Eye

If I would have known

How strong

You were prone to be

After some time of being diagnosed

With the big C

Then maybe

I would not have worried

As much

It makes me smile to see

That you have not lost your touch

Nor your smile

Sometimes while

In your presence, I stop and stare

Hoping that someday I too

Will reflect the strength I see in you.

Part Two:

Consciously Seeking for Myself

Chapter Sixteen:

sis b.k.a Still I Strive

Ra'Shell S. Maldon

If I focus on all I've lost
My soul would be somewhere lost
Searching for peace
While treading shits creek
Without a paddle in attempt to attain a piece
Of a dream I was sold
Instead I remind myself that if I hold
My faith long enough
The reward for doing so
Would be seeing my every blessing unfold
Even when the stress
Appears to be
Seemingly
More than I can bear
Without another soul present to share
These burdens I bare them publicly
Hoping that someone else will see
That they're not alone
And that there is nothing wrong
With being imperfect

My Mind's Eye

Yet still striving for perfection
Even when I'm at my lowest I hold my head high
To keep my crown sturdy
Pushing thirty
But not quite where you see fit for me to be
Still I strive unwilling to be beset
By life's obstacles so easily
I find it better to cut all strings
With those things
That threaten to bind
My mind
For I'm fully aware
That hardship doesn't last
I say a prayer
Inhale gas
And exhale my every care
Then soar to where
Frustrations cannot follow.

Ra'Shell S. Maldon

Chapter Seventeen:

My World Asunder

My Mind's Eye

My face is tear stained.

My eyes are grief-stricken.

My mind is clouded with uncertainty

and unanswered questions.

My heart is feeble, weary

and consumed with an irreversible affliction.

An affliction so relentless it refuses to be assuaged;

yet I smile.

Amid this emotional turmoil,

I smile knowing that although this affliction is enduring,

this emotional turmoil is fleeting

and shall soon subside

Father willing.

Chapter Eighteen:

This Woman's Growth

My Mind's Eye

I've triumphed over trials and tribulations as though His grace never left me

Not quite where I want to be

But apparently I'm exactly where He sees fit for me to be

At times it amazes me how far I've grown

Transitioned from the irresponsible girl you've known

Into a responsible woman

Who's still growing

He's changing me for the better

And it's showing

Although I'm knowing that I've come a long way

From being who I was yesterday

I realize that my journey is far from finished

Therefore I pray for my mind and spirit to be replenished daily.

Chapter Nineteen:

No Cry

My Mind's Eye

Rather than cry over spilt milk
I've learned it's best
To clean up the mess and allow my Creator
To sort out the rest
For crying
Only besets
And upsets my energy's
Consistency
Which ceases to flow consistently
The instant
My existence is perceived
Insignificant
After temporary needs are met
My existence is reduced
To a distant
Memory to forget
Then beget
At the convenience
Of another
Who finds inconvenience

Ra'Shell S. Maldon

In dealing
With feelings.

Chapter Twenty:

Misconception of Words

Ra'Shell S. Maldon

Words can never hurt me

How misleading

Because words are the reason

My mind is seething with insecurity That hinder me from being

A confident human being

But words can never hurt me

On the contrary

Words often hurt me

And often cause my self esteem

To desert me

Words had me convinced

That their narrow-minded perception of me

Could be true

So as I grew

I often longed to be

Anyone other than me

You see they ridiculed me

For being me

Declaring me

My Mind's Eye

A white girl trapped in

Melanin filled skin

Whose complexion was too light,

Mind was too bright,

And speech was too white

Much to my chagrin

This is where my self-hatred began

From my individuality, I ran

Seeking solace in a fictitious persona believing that if I pretended to be

The opposite of me

I could possibly be accepted

And no longer rejected

But acceptance

Under false pretenses

Could not numb my senses

And could not dissolve

My resolve

To resurrect my individuality

That lie dormant within

Ra'Shell S. Maldon

Words often discouraged
But rarely encouraged
Me to be comfortable in
The skin that I am in
But I had to learn to be somehow
So that now
I am able to regurgitate
My self hate
From within and begin
To embrace myself.

Chapter Twenty-One:

Breezes

Ra'Shell S. Maldon

Time frequently changes
But no matter the stages
Of this life
And no matter the weight
Of this strife
Unchanging you remain
Even in the midst
Of this pain
The gentle sway
Of your breezes that breathe my way
Whispering encouraging
Words
That halt discouraging
Thoughts
Keeping them at bay
If only to say
That misery
Doesn't deserve my company.

Chapter Twenty-Two:

Sometimes

Ra'Shell S. Maldon

Sometimes
These prophetic rhymes
Linger in this open mind
Escape loose lips
And unsettle steady ships
Anchored in obscurity
Because sometimes
Closed minds
Beget ignorance
That makes it difficult to see
Beyond what lies beneath
An orchestrated smile
That masks an emotional
And mental
Struggle within
Sometimes
My only refuge is the ink
In this pen
That I utilize
To materialize these feelings

My Mind's Eye

And thoughts
That threaten to consume my being
Sometimes
Finding the strength to continue being
Is more complexed than breathing.

Ra'Shell S. Maldon

Chapter Twenty-Three:

Expired Possibility

My Mind's Eye

Through experience I've learned

The best way

To escape a nightmare

Is to wake up

Still

I cannot will

Myself

To escape this nightmare

I am in

Feeling as if

I am sleepwalking

In a daze

Somewhere lost

In a haze

Someone pinch me

Because this reality feels

More surreal

Than real

Allowing my tears to spill

As I attest without delaying

Ra'Shell S. Maldon

To the saying
That everything
Isn't meant for everybody
Feeling as if
My body
Isn't meant to create
An unfortunate fate
That affirms the weight
Of creation
Is too much for me to bare
Fully aware
As life drains from my being
A sense of inadequacy
Leaves my being
Hollow inside
Yet my pride
Won't permit me
To seek comfort from he
Who couldn't possibly
Understand a grief

My Mind's Eye

He has yet to experience
No longer reveling in the relief
Of knowing
But growing weary
As the panic spreads fast
Catching up with
The paranoia from my past
That cast
Doubt on my ability
To adequately
Nurture our legacy to fully being
A sense of inadequacy
Manifests within my being
As stabbing pains
Jar me deeper into consciousness
Then course through my veins
Communicating the intensity
Of agonizing pain
Through receptors
From my stomach to my brain

Ra'Shell S. Maldon

As blue sheets

Are stained red

I struggle to silence

Pessimistic thoughts in my head

While muffling my screams

Through gritted teeth

As the possibility

Of me birthing our legacy ceases to flow

Along with the hope

Of a physician contradicting the fears

That now grow

Louder by the second.

Chapter Twenty-Four:

Self Destruction

Ra'Shell S. Maldon

The aftermath
Of relational strain
Fuels the resentment coursing
Through my veins
As hostile tears
Escape my eyes
Alluding to
The coming demise
Of kindred ties
Weakened
By the disrespect
And uncomfortable silence
That elicits a continual search for solace
As violence
Erupts within
I begin
Feeling like an explosive device
Waiting to implode
Reassemble
Then explode and unload

My Mind's Eye

My frustrations

Yet the urge

For self-mutilation

Was addressed with much hesitation

Until it became too great

To ignore

Resulting in me

Breaking on hardwood floors

Isolating myself

Behind closed doors

So no one can see

The destruction of me.

Ra'Shell S. Maldon

Chapter Twenty-Five:

Sea of Insecurities

My Mind's Eye

I am drowning in a sea of my own insecurities

In the midst of my quest to obtain clarity and happiness

I stumbled and I fumbled my confidence

Until it became lost in the abyss

Where my imperfections reside

And I shouldn't feel this sense of inadequacy I feel inside

For I am queen

Blessed to possess dominion over everything

Yet I cower away from my power

As if I were a peasant who never dared to do anything more than exist and obey

With great difficulty

I attempt to portray rationality

But in actuality

I'm not that good of an actor

Realizing that hurt from my past relationships serves as a relevant factor in my present relationship

I need to get a grip

Knowing that if I continue to slip in this sea of my own insecurities

Ra'Shell S. Maldon

He will loosen his grip on my heart

And sail away with his love without giving me a second thought.

Chapter Twenty-Six:

Destruction of a Broken-Hearted Soul

Ra'Shell S. Maldon

I came crashing down from up high
Clumsy me I fell off my cloud in the sky
With weary eyes that sat low
I felt my high fade
As sobriety crept up on me slow
In mid haze
I stumbled into my reflection
But when I gazed into the mirror's direction
I noticed too much of you in me
Then without warning
My emotions rebelled against my will
And started swarming
Soon after they escaped the security
Of their cage
Their aggression consumed my senses
As I rode their riotous
Wave of rage
Equipped with fist that went dashing
Into the mirror's glass
Then began clashing and repeatedly smashing

My Mind's Eye

Any likeness of you
Only ceasing after weary knuckles bled
And weary eyes shed
Irate tears
Hot with regret
I hate that I ever met you
More so I hate that my heart can't seem to
Forget you
Despite the countless times my mind
Has reminded it to
I guess my heart was too forgetful
Truth be told you were the one
I'm elated got away
Okay not really
In all honesty, you were the one
I thought would never stray
But would forever stay
In my life
For a lifetime
And forever be mine.

Ra'Shell S. Maldon

Chapter Twenty-Seven:

Creation to Creator

My Mind's Eye

Creator

I hope you incline Your ears

To hear me

I speak these words sincerely

When I say

I am no longer certain

Whether or not it makes sense

To continue to pray

Wait

What I mean to say

Is I hope You will make sense

Of this senseless tragedy

Because You see

Creator

As Your creation

I cannot begin to understand

Was it necessarily a part of Your plan

For him to depart us this way

Ra'Shell S. Maldon

More importantly
Before claiming his life
Did You consider the seeds
He leaves behind
And if so
Did You consider impact of his absence
In their lives
Now that they find
Themselves unable to embrace his presence

And how do we
A grieving family begin to
Reassure them
That everything
In this life happens for a reason
And that in due season
Everything
Will eventually be okay
Although not quite the way
As it was before

My Mind's Eye

Of this one thing
I am for sure
And if prayer changes
Anything
Then inner peace and strength are somethings
I pray for

Because Creator
Your creation is feeble
From fighting a spiritual war within
And longing for solitude again
I want to hide away
From the outside world today
Because this sense of hypersensitivity
That You instilled in me
Lately feels less like a blessing
And more like a curse
So now I am second guessing
The worth of being a righteous being.

Chapter Twenty-Eight:

Destination (Reconciliation or Separation)

My Mind's Eye

It's better this way I swear
Stay by my side
On this predestined ride
And sooner than later we'll arrive to where
We both desire to be

Countless times you've said you love me
Now I question the validity
Of that habitual declaration
Because if you love me
You wouldn't be contemplating separation
But without hesitation
You would be more supportive
And if you love me
No matter how bumpy the ride
You would be
Seated by my side
On this rickety locomotive

Until it steadily settles us

Ra'Shell S. Maldon

Somewhere
Further south of here
Or wherever
We decide to reside
And later plant our roots deeply
To provide stability
For our seeds
That succeed us

Put a little trust
And a little faith in me
Then without physically seeing
You will grasp my vision
Mentally seeing
That I possess the capability
To be the woman you need me to be
All I need from you is time

In the meantime
I need you to have my back

My Mind's Eye

And assume the role of my spine
While allowing me to do
The same for you

Believe in me
As I believe in you
And collectively
There will never be a storm too severe
For us to weather through
Because collectively
We can conquer
Any obstacle that seems
Unconquerable

This isn't a dream
That I am selling you
But my actions should be telling you
Of my determination to perfect
The art of making your every dream
Come true

Ra'Shell S. Maldon

And although I am imperfect
Our Creator created me
Perfectly imperfect
For you

As we approach this standstill
Before you decide
To vacate your place
By my side
And leave an empty space
I hope you will
Stand still
And set aside
Your pride
Long enough to will
Your heart not your eyes
To visualize
The triumph succeeding our journey.

Chapter Twenty-Nine:

Free Fall (Free for All)

Ra'Shell S. Maldon

Women like me are entitled to a title
That we rarely receive
In this generation, wearing your heart on your sleeve
Makes you susceptible to heartache for titles
Are as foreign as languages,
But the only language being spoken is body
Some women throw pussy freely
As if it is a hobby
And some men are not afraid
To catch
The pussy they throw,
But they are afraid
Of catching feelings
So they fuck frequently,
But rarely commit
Using past heartache
To justify embracing promiscuity
As they free fall into lust
As if love is nonexistent.

Chapter Thirty:

lol b.k.a Longing Out Loud

Ra'Shell S. Maldon

I am more than
Good enough
And even more than
The less than I used to settle for
Someday a worthy king
Or maybe someday a worthy queen
Will unconditionally adore me
Do anything for me
And proclaim me their everything
Then adorn me with a wedding ring
And a hyphen that precedes
Their last name.

My Mind's Eye

Author's Address

Dear Reader,

It is partially because of you
this soft-spoken poet
was encouraged to
use this poetry to find my voice
and now I rejoice
at the reality of being heard
and so, I thank you
for hearing me.

Peace & Positivity,
Ra'Shell S. Maldon

Ra'Shell S. Maldon

Connections To Ra'Shell

raapostrophe.blogspot.com

www.twitter.com/raapostrophe

www.instagram.com/raapostrophe

Author's Q&A

Who am I?

I am a (soft-spoken) starving artist, a high school graduate, but a college dropout who took an unorthodox route in life.

How would I describe myself?

Using three adjectives, I would describe myself as adventurous, analytical, and authentic.

Where am I from?

I was born an army brat in Tacoma, WA and raised in Montgomery, AL.

What am I passionate about?

I am passionate about my family, poetry, and writing.

What do I hope for?

I hope to leave an everlasting impression on any and every open mind that my influence touches (someday).

www.ingramcontent.com/pod-product-compliance
Lightning Source LLC
Chambersburg PA
CBHW072159100426
42738CB00011BA/2478